Finding Home

by Diane Jerome
Illustrated by Pat Paris

Editorial Offices: Glenview, Illinois • Parsippany, New Jersey • New York, New York
Sales Offices: Needham, Massachusetts • Duluth, Georgia • Glenview, Illinois
Coppell, Texas • Sacramento, California • Mesa, Arizona

For a long time, the Chumash Indians have lived along the coast of California. Many, many years ago, they lived in dome houses made of willow poles. They made beautiful baskets and canoes. They ate fish and shellfish, meat, pine nuts, and berries. Shells were important to the Chumash people. They used shells for fishing, for jewelry, and for money. But to Anacapa, a Chumash girl, seashells were just charming objects that she liked to collect.

One day, Anacapa was walking through her village. She waved and smiled at the women who were making their beautiful baskets. Some of the elders were getting ready to go fishing in their canoes. Everybody was busy, so Anacapa wandered down to the ocean to collect seashells for her family.

footprints

    When Anacapa left, the day was sunny. She followed the trail that led down to the ocean. She noticed some footprints and wondered if they were the prints of a coyote or a wolf. Anacapa turned when she heard a whisper. At first she thought it was her mother saying her name. Then she thought she heard her mother whispering to her, warning her not to wander so far away by herself. The sounds really were just the wind blowing through the trees. Then she heard a noise in the bushes.

    What could it be? she wondered. She could not wait until she was on the beach, away from the forest.

---

whisper: soft sound, soft speech

3

Anacapa thinks about how happy her family will be when she gives them the seashells.

When Anacapa arrived at the beach, she saw hundreds of seashells that sparkled in the sun. She decided that she would choose the seashells carefully. She imagined her mother laughing with delight and her father smiling. She inspected every seashell. Some were pink; some were white. She did not have a basket, so she had to be very particular about which shells to keep. She kept walking further down the beach to collect another beautiful shell. Anacapa was so busy finding the perfect seashells that she lost track of time.

---

particular: very careful; concerned with detail
lost track of: forgot about

lair

Hours passed, and the sun began to set on the ocean. As the sky grew dark, fog began to roll in, and Anacapa became very worried. She knew she could not find the path at night. She would have to look for a shelter to spend the night. She loved the ocean and the coast during the day, but she was afraid of what might be out there at night. Perhaps she would find a lair or a cave—a safe place where she could spend the night. She wondered if her parents were worried too. To ease her worries, she started to sing a song she made up.

The trees along the shore lands,
They rise up to the sun.
The sunrise on the ocean
Will soon light up the sky.
The waves out on the ocean,
They sing a lullaby.

---

lullaby: a calming song to put a child to sleep

Anacapa's parents tried to think of all the places where Anacapa might be.

　　Back in the village, Anacapa's parents were very worried. They asked the basket weavers and the canoe builders if they had seen Anacapa during the day. They wondered if anyone had seen which way she went. Everybody helped to look for her. They searched her favorite places near the redwood trees and near the fresh water creek. Hours passed, and the same fog that fell on the ocean was now creeping into the village. The fog did not stop Anacapa's family from looking for her. They searched all night but did not find her.

At last, in the morning, the sky slowly grew bright. The rays of sunlight danced on Anacapa's tired eyes, and she awoke. Anacapa had not eaten any food the night before, so she was very hungry. She stopped to gather berries and dig for clams. She remembered how her father always used his hands when he caught shellfish, and she did the same. She would tell her parents how she remembered her lessons, and they would be proud. But then she realized that she must hurry home. Her parents would be worried. Her mother always told her to stay close to the village. She would be in trouble!

Anacapa looked up at the sky. She saw a condor soaring high, gliding in the breeze. She knew condors were considered a good sign. This condor would lead her to the trail with the whispering trees. Soon she would be home. She ran along the beach as though she had wings too. As she approached the village, she had mixed feelings. She had enjoyed her adventure near the sea, but she was also nervous. Her parents would scold her.

She was looking down at the trail when she heard her mother's voice. It was not a whisper, but a loud shout of joy. As they hugged each other, they laughed and cried—tears of happiness and tears of fear. Everyone was happy Anacapa was home again.

---
gliding: flying smoothly, moving in a smooth manner